for the Spirit

SHEREEMA DUMAS

NEWMAN SPRINGS PUBLISHING
320 Broad Street
Red Bank, NJ 07701

First originally published by Newman Springs Publishing 2022

Cover Design by Saa DeBlasio

ISBN 978-1-68498-425-1 (Paperback)
ISBN 978-1-68498-421-3 (Digital)

Printed in the United States of America

To all my beautifully good-spirited
children and theirs, thank you!

Contents

A Different Path (12/08/02)

The rays of the sun shone bright
Even through the dark of night
The moonbeams held all the light
To give me a brand-new sight.
This never-ending sight led me a different way
Constantly weaving all throughout the night and day
Tunnels of darkness for lengths unknown only faith could say
Dreams in all their mystery gave me answers without delay.

Love in all its splendor is priceless, so I've been told
I traveled long and waited for true love to take its hold
Now finally I know the essence of this love so bold
It strengthens me as this different path continues to unfold.

A Long Journey (11/17/98)

The longest journey I ever walked
Was somewhere I don't want to be.
It took me down inside my gut
And wrenched me to and fro.
The sharklike teeth ripped at my heart
And took me even lower.
The pain, the agony, the fire.
I feel this must be hell—it is.
The longest journey I ever walked
Was deep inside of me.

A Man I Once Loved (07/19/01)

A man I once used to love
Did horrid things to me
I loved him quite completely
Despite the things he did
I'd cry and wonder why
He used to take his hands to do
Things not at all endearing
Sometimes his hands would find
     A place around my throat or face
Then other times it was his size 12
     That pressed upon my chest
Yet even though I found myself
     Still in love with him
Hoping always against hope that things
     Would be all right
Trying hard to please my man, so I'd be
     Worthy of his love
The words he used, he chose them well
They made me question who I was
I made excuses for his actions and blamed myself
I'd hold some ice upon my face to soothe
     A meeting with his hand
I'd hide at home in bed so no one would ever know
But years just passed with my love growing weary
Wanting just to end the pain that now consumed me
I tried sometimes to end it all, to make the pain just STOP!
But never could I succeed
I tried hard to change my life
To take control of it

But a man that I once loved stood
In my way
It's been years since I have loved him
And I've made that very clear
But somehow, I'm not free; the walls
Are all still there
I don't know what it will take to break
Those walls and set me free
Of a man I once loved but did not love me.

A Retreat (08/01/01)

Just look at the word *retreat*,
To me it's a joke that can't be beat.
Don't remember being free,
Long enough to have time for me.
Do we treat ourselves again,
To loneliness we feel within?

A Road Not Yet Traveled (06/02/09)

My journey through life has taken me down many a road
Some roads have been smooth
With experiences to soothe
Some have been bumpy
Leaving one to feel grumpy
Adrift on the sea
Struggling just to be me
But now my journey has brought me to a road untraveled.
The road fresh and new
Will it lead to something true?
Will I feel I've grown?
Climb to greater heights unknown?
Yes, I will explore
And live like never before.
This road may not yet be traveled
But its point of entry is upon me, so I shall not linger more.

A Show (08/01/01)

On my way to a show
One I never have been
A celebrity host
With some guest I don't know.
Rode the bus to the train
"E" to Fiftieth Street
Bus to Tenth Avenue
Walk three blocks without strain.

Give ticket for Montel
Then I'm given a seat
To view all the action
Will have you so compel
To turn on your tele
And watch you cheer aloud
The celebrity host
Whom you can see daily.

A Silence (2008)

A silence engulfed me in a way that was almost numbing. The obvious sounds around were muted by my thoughts. My thoughts were struggling to override each other in an attempt to maintain control. Control the tears, control the tremors, control that may seem natural at this point to do. *I must be strong* was my greatest thought. *I must do this for Mommy.* I told myself that if I should have the nerve to request nothing less for myself, then how dare I not have the strength to do it for the woman who brought me into this world, who taught me to believe in the Almighty in the matter in which I do?

How could I abandon all that was given to me through her and all that I am because of the fear of…what? Afraid to touch the lifeless body of the woman who wiped my tears and nursed me; afraid that my eyes may be offended by what it views, when my mother taught me that there was beauty in all things and that beauty was in the eyes of the beholder; afraid of being traumatized at seeing such a finale of my mother, that this is what I might remember rather than the mommy whom I loved?

At some moment in time of which I do not know precisely when, like a subtle breeze that sways suddenly where there was none, there was a calmness that came over me. The fear had disappeared, and before me were only the love for my mother and the beauty of our existence. There before me was a sense of pride in a way I had never experienced before. Watching that peace transfer to my mother's face with a glowing light around her was like none other. This peace and profound wisdom had replaced all fear.

As we stood before her at her final resting place and felt the cool breeze blow around us and through our legs, as we looked up at the skies that had suddenly cleared, showing the heavens that awaited her, I knew. I knew that she got all that she wanted and that we had done all that we needed to do. The heavens had opened themselves up for her for all of us to see. Our prayers continued as they covered that final place, which was shaded by a tree that seemed to bow in her honor. The Lord and all His creation were pleased.

Dear Lord, here lies my mother; into your arms she will be received. The wind blew in blue skies, high white fluffy clouds, a beautiful sunset, and a procession to lead her to the gateway of heaven.

A Simple Dream (03/01/05)

All I ever wanted, I saw in a dream
Sunny days, smiles, and dancing in a stream.
Pitter-patter of little feet, four or more.
Each and every one, wonders to adore.
A dream of loving life, with all my family
One that has been tried but unsuccessfully.
The dream fades quickly as the years pass away,
Prints in the sand have a separate say.
Struggling to hold the dream, to steal, one chance
A simple dream come true so we can all advance.

Always Late! (10/17/01)

Some people are always late
    Rushing to and fro
        Always making others wait
Some people are always late
    Learning lessons slow
        Always playing with their fate
Some people are always late
    Borrowing time here and there
        Always owing at a rate
Some people are always late
    Changing their relationships
        Always needing a clean slate
Some people are always late
    Missing life all their lives
        Always hurting their mate
Some people are always late
    Delaying day and night
        Always being bait

At Last! (04/16/88)

I look before me and watch a shadow
Engulfing all the light.
I close my eyes, and puzzled, I behold
The shadow even in the night.

Some strange and uncontrollable urge
Wants to draw me close,
But fear of its unknown force
Forbids me most.

And yet and still, my heart beats fast.

To forge right on ahead,
Through hills of thorns and fogs of fear,
Endure the pain and erase the gloom,
To seize this shadow and take control.

No longer shall I allow this shadow
To haunt my very soul,
But pray The Lord that all is best,
And shine a light so very bright no shadows
                                        Ever cast.

At last! We feel the calm in heart
And still tranquility.

The shadow is gone! I feel the peace.
A soul's at rest. At last!

AMEN.

Be with Me (01/23/01)

Walk with me throughout my journey
Talk with me throughout my life.
Laugh with me in spite of grief
Cry with me in spite of pride.
Feel with me my every joy
See with me my every pain.
Be with me.

Blessings (06/09/05)

Hidden behind every door is a blessing
Around every corner is a blessing
At every crossroad we choose our blessing
We go about our lives struggling to make sense
The everyday occurrences of
Getting up...Washing up
Getting dressed...Doing our hair
Walking...Talking...Thinking...Breathing
In and of themselves, they are each a blessing
Sometimes the path we're on, chosen or forced upon
We struggle through
Pain...Anger...Rage
And then hopelessness
Surrounded by absolute darkness
There is always light
The choice is ours; it's called "Free Will"
A blessing in itself
To fight...To be strong...To rise above
To see beyond the trees
To learn...To grow
Teach others what we've come to know
Use our struggle...pain...and agony
To turn things all around
Reap the blessings of your survival
Then be blessed for doing so.

Blind Faith (10/03/01)

I don't understand why things keep going wrong
It happens each time I try to be strong
No matter where I go or what I do
My successes are always few.
I always watch for signs to lead my way
And pray The Lord I not be led astray.
Sometimes my goal is clear what must be done
Taking away from all my fun.
Then when I believe I have got it right,
My agenda is set, and everything looks bright.
Soon vision fades, so I'm lost in a maze
Running around in just a daze.
Promises made to myself help me today
To a path, not even knowing the way.
Somehow, it's just blind faith that guides through
Helping me breathe and feel anew.

Chance to Say (10/17/01)

It isn't very often
I have the chance to say
How very much I love you
In every possible way.

I know you don't believe
This could even be
But I hate to tell you
I just must disagree.

Changes (06/08/07)

Some people want to do things all the time the same
Some people never do anything the same
Some people have a constant regiment
Some people believe periodic change is profound

Some people wait to see what others are doing
Some people never do things like others
Some people wait for tomorrow, which never comes
Some people just live for the here and now

Some people change quickly throughout life as does time
Some people make few changes in their lives.

Concessions (03/27/11)

Here lost among all the other stones I lay
Wondering how I will be seen from all that are on top
I struggle to stand out despite we're all the same
Some think that they are greater just because of their size
Others just keep you pinned locked in just one place
Daily it's a struggle just getting equal access
Like all the ones on top
But time has shown that some things never change
It's concession time to just lay among the others
And be seen or not
What concessions will you make in your life
To manage all your strife
Do you feel no need to make adjustments,
For few acknowledgments?
You'll make your troubles rife.

Countdown (12/31/06)

At least once a year, everyone stops to reflect on all that has passed
Reliving what should have, could have, would have been if,
Only to acknowledge what actually was

Regrets some will experience during those last hours of the year
Blessings abundant, others will rejoice in prayer
Yet all still will be asking themselves why

The question will be "Why did I not have what I wanted most?"
All will ponder what they did or did not do right
Knowing it was too late to change anything

It was a countdown again for yet another year to be upon us,
Giving way to thoughts of depression and those of joy
With new declarations at the final countdown

Dance (03/08/05)

I hear music ever so often, playing in my ear
That music makes my fingers *rap-pa-tap* out the beat
Then suddenly my movement changes to both of my feet
Body swaying to and fro without a single care.

Soft, gentle music I listen to and smile
That music makes my heart flutter in utter ecstasy
Quite calm and soothing, hypnotized all the while
I close my eyes to see my perfect fantasy.

Dancing in my head to all my melodic tunes
That music makes my soul reach heights it's never gone
Twirling all around me, lifting like balloons
My spirit just keeps dancing like a graceful swan.

Suddenly another tune plays loudly in my head
That music makes my head bob up and down
Yes, to all the joyfulness upon the paths I tread
At last, to dance again without a single frown.

Day by Day (2015)

Day by day
I think and pray
Don't know what to do
Keeps me blue
Must find my way
Make me feel anew
Day by day
Time passes...Where it goes, I know not where
Time passes...Nothing stays the same
Time passes...Support to move along

Doesn't Really Matter (08/16/87)

Lives have touched
Souls have met
Paths have crossed
But the sun won't set.

Miles I traveled
Mountains I climbed
Dreams I lived
But the clock won't chime.

Has it been a year
Or maybe just a day?
Has it been an hour?
Oh! I dare not say.

It doesn't really matter
How much time has passed.
The only points to gather
Your dreams that truly last.

Emancipation Day (10/18/01)

Today was the day I have been waiting
    For so very long.
Today was the day my life was
    Supposed to change.
Things the way they used to be were
    Going to be no more.
Things the way they used to be would
    Sing a brand-new song.

Such hope of new tomorrows brings
    To me glee.
But there was nothing different
    At all about the day
The sun came up…I heard the
    Birds chirp.
There were no banners waving…
    I AM FREE!

Somehow it really was not
    Quite the way I thought
All was rather quiet in a strange,
    Peculiar way.
A subtle kind of numbness that
    Seemed to lead me through.
Which lulled me from my memories of
    Battles I have fought.

What happened to the fanfare
                    That should have been for me?
To celebrate emancipation:
                    To shout to the world, "I'M FREE!"
Huh! Some Emancipation Day.

Everlasting Love (02/13/01)

Who would have guessed that
Our paths would cross again?
Who would have guessed that
Our hearts be joined once more?

I only know you are the
Morning and evening.
I only know you are the
Energy within.

Today and every day, you are
My open door.
Today and every day, you are
My love.

Faceless Friends (10/08/06)

Somewhere between the business of our daily routine
Sometime between the minutes spent listening to your pleas
A chorus begins to play a song into my ear.

Some would set their tearful woes to a symphonic beat
Others would set their frustration with rhythmic soliloquies
A song begins to paint pictures of their tales of woe.

The brush would rise with quick precision and detail
The outline drawn would be complete—all except there's
No face
A picture formed inside my mind is of my faceless friend.
Many faceless friends fill my heart with their melodic tunes.

Feeling Like a Fool (10/03/01)

Here I sit beside the pool
Bathing in the sun
Asking myself how could I be such
    "A fool"?
The sun is direct and warm
Cooling in the water
Trying to forget, the swiftness of
    The storm.
Here I sit in anxiousness
Without a single clue
Oh, how to weather inside of me this constant
    Foolishness.
The sun is strong and high
Praying, I ask for help
To cool my uneasy spirit, and never mind
    Asking why.

Finding Peace (09/02/04)

Peace is a quiet friend who makes no announcements
It does not speak or make any sounds to alert its presence
Instead, it waits patiently to be happily discovered
Peace is something we all want to experience
Some will spend a lifetime in search of it but with no success
Others will bask in glory and ecstasy when the quest ends
Peace is not something to see on the horizon
Nor is it any unsuspecting face in a crowd we gaze
But rather the overwhelming feeling deep inside of us

Forgive Myself...How? (10/21/01)

Who will help turn life around to make
a brand-new start?
Who will help make me forget the pain
I caused each one?
What was I not doing right to make
you understand?
What was I living on Earth to do
for anyone?
Where did life take the turn to the
path I was on?
Where did life throw away ALL that
was worth living?
When were we supposed to become as one?
When were we engulfed with all
this suffering?
How do I forgive myself for all the
pain I've caused?
How do I stop committing crimes
against my soul?
Why was I so blind to things
before my own eyes?
Why was I so ignorant of what
love really was?
How can I forgive myself for
taking such abuse?
How can I repair the damage
that already has been done?
Then finally but most of all
Who will help me...FORGIVE MYSELF?

Forgiven!

I know I must forgive myself
I will not be my judge.
I know I must forgive myself
I will release all guilt.
I know I must forgive myself
I will not be ashamed.
I know I must forgive myself
I will not live in fear.

Change, for me, will only happen
When I hold on to no grudge.
Change, for me, will only happen
When I strengthen the house I built.
Change, for me, will only happen
When I live as I proclaim.
Change, for me, will only happen
When I wash away the tears.

I know then...I am FORGIVEN!

Getting Back to Your Roots (09/20/01)

Life begins with a journey of a lifetime.
Where it leads depends on us.
At first, our journey is smooth,
Making our mobility a quick rise.
Enter some hills that we must climb,
With several crossroads to be chosen.
We choose a path that leads us away
From our ultimate goal in life.
Wandering and searching for the right path,
We find ourselves in total darkness.
We cannot see.
Even what presents itself directly in front of us,
Our vision is clouded.
A voice deep within speaks to us.
If we listen to our inner spirit faithfully,
It shows the right path and lights the way for us.
The journey back into the light is not an easy one,
But most precisely leads us to our ultimate goal:
Proving our worthiness to The Lord.
Most definitely, this path takes us on a journey
Back to the innocence of our birth and who we are.
This journey in life gets us back to our roots,
Where we belong...
Where we belong...
Amen!

Goody-Goody (10/03/01)

I once was a goody-goody;
At least that's what they say.
Always doing right, all I did was pray.

No way could I ever perceive
That life would take a twist
To almost lose my soul, who would believe?

I try to have faith do a turn
Get my life directed
Away from the past, wiser that I learn.

Today I know my soul is good.
I always try to pray,
Freeing my spirit, just the way it should.

Now goody-goody's not my name.
A new me has emerged.
Stronger, wiser—I'm nowhere near the same.

Gut Feelings (What Lies Within) (05/28/05)

Somewhere deep within me, a feeling is being born
Many have arrived before, each unique in their own way
Yet still it may resemble another from before
Sometimes the feeling makes me warm and cuddly inside
Other times, I anxiously await to see how it will grow
On some few occasions, I know right from its birth
All its characteristics and fear the very worst
Very quickly some do grow to show their true nature
Few are born instantaneously, wise beyond their time
But no matter what their nature, I've learned to appreciate
What my gut feelings mean is what lies within me.

Gypsy (09/17/01)

I've been a gypsy for a long time...
I have abstained from the abstract gesture with gentle but genuine
giddy gibberish
until the abeyance of one's ability abdicates the abnormal, abject acumen
To be abashed by the absurdity and abort, not abide, for final absolution.
This germane gest abnegates a gypsy and absolves me.

I am not a gypsy anymore.

Happy Birthday, K'mari (08/15/07)

K'mari, with your eyes so bright, today is your special day.
I know how you loved to have Grandma sing a song her special way
Or have me read and animate *Goldilocks and the Three Bears*.
You seemed to understand all that we did without tears.

Born wise beyond years with understanding eyes,
Big, bold, beautiful brown eyes that dazzled with much surprise
Peaceful not a crybaby you were all the time
K'mari, my daughter, my love, my heart so sublime.

When you laugh, I see joy…
Your smile lights up my day.
Knowing what I say…
All for me to enjoy.
Your facial expressions…
Make me giggle…
With such impressions…
I start to wiggle.

K'mari, as you always felt my presence, I am here.
We take this time to celebrate YOU this year.
Born to me at 5:25 p.m.
I'll always remember, my precious gem.

HAPPY BIRTHDAY, K'MARI!

Flowers, one of God's delicate beauties
They sway in the gentle breeze
Petals open and close
Flowers blossom and goes
Colors adorn all their leaves
The earth is amused at how they dance
You, to me, are my flower
Delicate and rare
A beauty to share
I laughed with joy that you were here.
Happy birthday!

Hard to Believe (10/17/01)

It's hard to believe
Where life has taken me
Never did I expect it to end this way
But my childhood dreams of
Happily ever after
Never came to be

I married you so very much in love
You promised me
To give me all my heart's desire
Make my dreams come true
Instead, you took my heart and soul
And I couldn't see
I gave you babies
I dried their tears
I worked your business
Whatever your dreams were then
It drained my spirit
I lived in fear

I tried to change
To meet your needs
Only to still be wrong in everything I did
Couldn't figure out
What was wrong with me
Was it any of my deeds?

I couldn't seem to please you
No matter what I did
I just cried the night away
That life was not for me
Escape to death
Took an open bid

Years would come
And years would go
Living became very unimportant
A torturous event
Until I had a dream
One that helped to show

How I could have my dream
It gave me a key
Of what my life had become
The cycle of lies
The cycle of pain
I could stop and be free

It's hard to believe
Where life has taken me
Never did I expect it to end this way
But my childhood dreams of
Happily ever after
Never came to be

I've used my key
And now some things
Are falling into place for me
Now I live to love
And welcome what it brings

It's hard to believe
Where life has taken me
Never did I expect it to end this way
But now life's offering
Something new
A brand-new me.

Harmonious Hymn (05/23/06)

Hear harmonies of happiness
Hoist hope to heighten horizons
Honor heroism as one's heritage
Hesitate not to hale holiness
However, heredity holds health
Heed herbal and honey in heaps.
Humble your heart to helpfulness
Humor hypocrisy with hospitality
Have home a haven for all humanity
Hold honesty as a halo
Hunger most for a healthy head
Hum a hymn harmoniously

Harmony (03/01/01)

When you choose to play
Any...
Symphony,
You will see, we will
Always be...
In perfect...
Harmony.

Heaven Calling (11/03/06)

Born to this temporal world
No trials, no tribulations
No worries, no fears
Only heaven calling.

No pain, no heartbreak
No diseases, no stress
No anxiety
Only heaven calling.

Held, nursed, rocked, kissed, loved
In this temporal world
Angels come and take you to
The spiritual world.

How blessed I feel to have been
A part of your world.

Hope to Be Free (06/2002)

The day I was married was the day hope began.
The day I divorced was the day hope died.
Supposedly this day I was emancipated,
    First as a woman and then as a FREE woman.
Before, there was food in the cupboards and the fridge
    Now the cupboards and fridge are both bare.
Emancipation—what an interesting thought…
    To live our lives as we best see fit.
But much like the slaves who were imprisoned by their masters,
    Freedom was NOT felt.
Disguised as new hope, the day I divorced was only a new prison
    Supported with subtle words…
        That sneak into my head like a thief.
I know that this prison is only my mind playing tricks on me.
Hopefully, I will soon know new hope and really be FREE.

How Do You Roll? (05/17/15)

Which way do you roll?
Do you use guides to lead the way,
or do you allow yourself to go astray?
Which way do you roll?
Do you always take control,
or do you struggle with delay?
Which way do you roll?
Do you have any say
on what's your goal?
How do you roll?

How I've Grown (04/12/01)

It amazes me how much
I've grown.
Yet there's so much
yet unknown.
One at a time, I live
each day,
for divine guidance to
show the way.
My life seems lost with
only a clue,
but I pray each day to
start anew.
I grow each day a little
more,
the blessings that come
I can't ignore.

I Pray for You (04/26/89)

My thoughts I have that you are there,
My dreams I have I hope to share.
Too many years have come and passed,
But time has seen that love can last.
Be there to hear my plea for you,
Be there to see my heart is true.
I pray that when you hear my cries,
You will come and renew our ties.
The Lord is good, The Lord is great,
I pray The Lord; I will not wait.
Amen.

I'll Smile, I'll Live (05/23/89)

My heart may be aching, but I won't die;
I'll live to see the leaves change colors, fall
And then grow back again.
I'll live to see my children grow up and
Make me a grandma.
I'll live to sing praises to The Lord up
High above.
I'll live to feel the glory of His strength
Within my soul.

My heart may be aching, but I won't cry;
I'll smile at all the other smiling faces
That pass me here and there.
I'll smile at hills adorned with pretty flowers.
I'll smile up to the heavens as space
Engulfs me everywhere.
I'll smile because I wake to find still
Another day.

I'm Smiling (07/17/01)

Today I smiled for more than just one moment.
I smiled for some incredible reason the entire day.
There was no moment I felt the pain of circumstance.
At no time did my mind wander off to lands I hate to be.
Instead, I found myself content with subtle joy
Just enjoying the busyness of all I gazed upon,
Watching things new to me unfold throughout.
Amazed in silence, smiling within disbelief a day should
Pass
Without distress.
I can't believe I'm smiling.
I'm actually smiling...

In Awe of a Beautiful Rainbow

Only a year ago, it seemed as though the storm would never end. I found myself weeping silently to myself as to not let on to anyone of my emotional state. Though I struggle to protect myself from some very thunderous weather, never would I believe what I behold now.

There among the colors of this rainbow is my true love. Nestled are my children and grandchildren. Woven into all these are my sense of pride and desire to live as I've never lived before. This magnificent rainbow—I am in awe.

Finally, I find myself with an appetite for longevity. No longer do I sense the pain of yesterday. Instead, I dream of tomorrows and all that life can be. Adventure seeker that I am, I feel that I have found my pot of gold at the end of this rainbow.

Only last year, my heart took a beating yet again. But here I am today with a love I've never known before. Its brilliance lights up my life in such incredible ways. Never has any man cared so dutifully for me in every way.

Nothing short of miraculous that I can truly say, my prayers have been answered beyond my wildest dreams. Because of those answered prayers, I dare to dream again. This time, I believe that it really is possible that someone like me could be in awe of a beautiful rainbow.

Journeys (1980s)

It's very strange how life unfolds itself. What may appear to be a lost cause may suddenly blossom into one's most glorious dreams come true.

I look back upon my life—its ups and downs, its tragedies, its times of joy—and realize that it has really been quite full of what life is truly all about.

My trials, I imagine, have been no greater than most others', even though within myself they have been a living nightmare. The strength, which I have continually drawn upon, has not been within me but some entity much greater than myself.

I remember as I sat upon the windowsill of my bedroom I'd travel to a place unknown, far beyond the stars. I'd feel comfort in this restless place, and I'd move about at will, wandering to and fro and then back home again. There always was a sense of peace when I'd indulge. Now somehow, I seem to have lost the luxury of time to indulge.

These pillars I have watched
These anchors I have launched
The peace my heart requires
Stay locked in boundless walls.

Endless journeys with no path
Sightless visions that one beholds
Then reality slaps you once, then twice.

K'mari (11/03/06)

K'mari, who were you?
You were a little bundle of joy
Precious in every way to all who looked upon you.
K'mari, what's your purpose?
Your purpose was to bring the light,
Touch souls so deep within the heart and feel its beat.
K'mari, why did you leave?
You left because The Lord called you
To remind us all to always remember Him.
To know we were given a true blessing,
The gift of life, in K'mari.

Life and Faith (06/17/00)

Life unfolds in many ways,
Life unfolds in ways unknown.
Life beholds through rays of light,
Life beholds through dark of night.
Faith unfolds when life is there,
Faith beholds when life is here.
Life and Faith—the two are told
Will make us strong in every way.

Life

As it presents
Itself...
Is sad.
LIFE
As it promises
To be...
Is hope!

Loneliness (06/07/05)

Is it loneliness if you're in a crowded room and cannot see
A single one?
Is it loneliness if you're sitting all alone but your thoughts crowd
you
So you cannot move?
Or is it loneliness when you busy yourself with everyone except
The special one?

Loneliness wears a mask, disguising its true self.
Loneliness is like a disease desperately in need of a cure.
It's when you cannot stand to be all by yourself.

Or is your mind and body just playing tricks on you—
To feel but not be felt, to hold but not be held, or to love
But not be loved?
Is it enough to have someone to love if their presence is only
mindful
But not in the flesh?

Mankind's March (09/03/06)

The manipulated manner in which mankind
Maximized methods of manufacturing mechanical
Manpower is, as a matter of fact, a makeup of a
Make-believe meaningless mirror of malfunctioning
Monopoly on mankind.

Mass mayhem masks itself as the new millennium
Means maintaining mankind. Marching marvels
Make mazes of momentous markets manifesting
Mankind's mission.

My Dearest Friend (11/18/98)

My dearest friend, whose presence is forever near,
Fills me up with special thoughts,
Takes me back to times and places,
Where life was lived each day without a care.
My dearest friend, whose words articulate compassion,
Soothes me when the river floods,
Returns me back to solid ground,
Where life is lived with many less frustrations.

My World (06/09/00)

My world is a place deep inside my soul.
My world is a place with misty days
and muddy nights.
My world is a place no one really knows.
My world feels like a heart taking its last beats.
My world feels like a child lost in a jungle
and scared.
My world feels like the wind in a typhoon.
My world moves how one does without a home.
My world moves how a carousel does
and is never ending.
My world moves and lives within me only.

New Chapter

Amazing how we get to a certain point in our lives and are told we are all grown up now and are now on our own to figure things out. Then some years later, we realize the reason the other grown-ups older than us could not tell us more is either they did not know the answers themselves or they suffered from a very inevitable disease called CRS, which the elders have happily informed me means "Can't remember sh——t!"

Yes, that's right. I said it just as she told me. It was hard to believe what she was saying, but it was funny as heck because it was so true. I couldn't believe she hit the nail on the head without me telling her that I couldn't remember what I had done with my keys for days. I knew I didn't lose them, but I couldn't remember where I put them to save my life.

Whatever this new chapter is, it definitely has a lot more positive promises than any of my other chapters. Most times, I didn't have a clue where I was going to end up next. The challenges were great, the roads were rough, and the journeys were all uphill (more like climbing a mountain), but somehow, I survived. I would not say that I got up the mountain, but I would describe it as more like slipping and sliding back down the mountain to start over on a different track. Now I am starting a "new chapter" of my life on an even, smooth path with nothing but positive possibilities.

Will I now have the ability to share my newfound wisdom with the next who enters their new chapter?

New Life (06/28/05)

Nestled inside of me
Safe as it can be
Is new life at its best.

Taking shape deep within
An unknown soul thrives
Nourished with my spirit
And strengthened with my love.

Showing off its strength and size
It kicks and bounces to each task.
Sometimes it sleeps when I do
And often awakens when I'm not.

But playing lets its presence be known
Too big for the space it resides
It journeys to meet
The one who kept it safe.

Now to be held in my arms
The new life that came from me.

Not My Choice (06/28/05)

It was NOT my choice to be where
I am today.
It was NOT my choice to do what
I do today.
It was NOT my choice to know what
I know today.
It was NOT my choice to see what
I see today.
It was NOT my choice to feel what
I feel today.
It was NOT my choice to be who
I am today.
But since all these have
Come to be,
Then I choose to be the ME
I have become.

Ode to a Lost Love (11/17/98)

A part of me is dying,
A part of me has died.
I wish that all my tears,
Could wash away my fears.

A part of me is dying,
The why is still not too clear.
I pray for resolution,
To end this mass confusion.

A part of me is dying,
A love so deep and pure.
I thought it never-ending,
But life's just descending.
A part of me is dying,
All say that it's okay.
I need to live life anew,
And find a fresh point of view.

A part of me is dying,
Only joys will I regret.
I won't look back and grieve,
Only praise what I will receive.
A part of me is dying,
But a part is being born.

Office Medley (02/20/88)

I sit and bathe among the pens
The paper hills and bills to send.
I soothe my mind with sounds of rings
And pleas of warmth each caller sings.
I sigh. At last! A moment free
Of paper, pens, and think "Just me!"
A numbness sets all about
Sitting frozen, wearing a pout.
Just drifting in space, thinking of
All to be done.
While sitting in place, not doing
A one.
Then *rrring*, to hear
That favorite song.
Brings me back to my
Paper, pens, I belong.

Only Once a Week (07/17/01)

Today, I met a special lady
One I've often seen in court
A familiar place I visited
Only once a week.
She sat upon the bench
Strong yet regal
Listening and judging all who
Came before her.
Even though this place
Was quite fictional
She portrayed her strength
And compassion,
A strong Black woman.
I sit before my television
Only once a week
To glimpse this special lady
I only met today
She shows the world
In her own way
How things should really be.
A message to be heard
And practiced all throughout the land
Many may hear, but
Who is really listening
To one special lady
Only once a week?

Orlando (07/01/91)

Here lies the body of a gentle soul
To please his mother was his major goal
Orlando James was his name
To finish school was his only aim
But time did come and end it all
He had to answer to a greater call

Here walked Orlando in York each day
Smiling and friendly in his special way
All did know him as Orlando James
Making his mom proud he did remain
But time did come to say goodbye
Leaving all who knew him asking why

Here spoke Orlando to everyone
Kindness and warmth were all that he had
Said and done
We will remember Orlando James
In our hearts he'll remain the same
His time had come we do declare
Thank God for Orlando and his loving care.

Path Made of Faith (10/17/01)

I knew one day I'd see the sun
I'd feel all its warmth
It lends itself to light the way
Out from my dark past.
I walk along an unknown path
I cannot see at all
This path of mine is one of faith
Composed of hopes and dreams.
I emerged from a tunnel
Winding in and out
That closes tight behind me
Can't look or turn back.
I knew one day the sun would shine
Without a shadow of a doubt
It drew me out from below
Knowing not just how.
Now I see the light
Now I feel the warmth
Now I walk the path
The path that's made of faith.

Patience? (01/23/01)

Patience eludes me
I walk in quiet silence
Stumbling in the dark
Desperately trying to find my way.
It seems as if each step
Plunges me further into night
Until I am blind, totally without insight
And then, at last, the dawn of a new day.
Now patience is my virtue.

Peanut Pay (06/02)

Packing bags, saying "Thank you,"
Just working, standing on my feet.
All throughout the day,
People smile, some people bark,
Then some just want to make you laugh,
While having their say.
Returning items daily,
Placing back on the shelves for sale,
Some for work or play.
Stocking and moving items
Displays attracting more buyers
As they go their way.
Closing time, at last we're done
We count our sales for all our work,
Then our peanut pay!

Pouring Salt (10/20/04)

Totally torn, my guts ripped out while I still...
Toil to breathe while gasping secretly...
Holding the tears desperately while water runs...
Uncontrollably down my frowning face while waiting...
A number to be called, my case—I'm summoned, and I rise...
My shaky legs barely support my advance, then...
My name is called, and my pain, my pride, my life is...
Sentenced to yet another death in just two minutes...
Weak with fear of what I did to dare to tell the truth...
Now I return to where it started: home.
But instead of feeling a sense of relief or even peace...
As I face my abuser, I feel the burning of pouring salt into my open wounds.
No justice was received in any way...
Only humiliation, degradation, and total insecurity...
Oh, that's right! I was seeking refuge from these things my lover made me feel...
But instead, I felt even more hopeless before a courtroom judge.

Pouring salt when one's in pain will never help to heal.
Healing body, heart, and soul will pave a way to hope.

Promises (2006)

PROMISES for better or for worse

PROMISES to rescue one

PROMISES to be a knight in shining armor

PROMISES to be his one true love

PROMISES to obey and honor

PROMISES to protect one

PROMISES to be a queen to Prince Charming

PROMISES, PROMISES, PROMISES.

Pudding (07/30/01)

Pudding—soft, smooth, brown...
Lusciously intoxicating.
Pudding—engulfing all the caverns of my walls...
Sinfully teasing.
Pudding—wet, cool, light...
Exultingly fulfilling.

Reflections (06/07/05)

In a moment of silence, I pause and recollect all the aspects
of my life
I close my eyes as I reflect upon things that brought me pain
A frown came upon my face as I continued to reflect
Then choosing not to stay so quite severe, I reflect upon what
made me
proud.

Suddenly, that frown is gone to find a smile that fills me up with joy
I continue to reflect as to how I came to be where I am now
But once again, that frown crept in and stole my smile, and
filled my heart
with sadness.

Shine (04/12/07)

Today is your day to shine
Roses adorn you on their vine
Red colors spray throughout your path
All for a perfect photograph
Smiles it brings on our faces
Moving to different places
Shadows everywhere are longer
Creating illusions stronger
Enjoy the light of this day
Feel the warm breeze blowing your hair
Watch the leaves dance as the trees sway
Close your eyes, and you will be there
Awake and relive your dreams
Roses become your living theme
Red is your color, oh so bright
Enlightening us with foresight.

Sleepless (06/04/00)

My being awaits your presence.
My body longs for your caress.

The silence of the night rings in my head.
The darkness rocks the night to bed.

Yet quietly I rise and move all throughout,
Hoping to conclude my never-ending doubt.

My mind drifts to and fro.
My heart aches only to know.

The silence of the night is lonely.
The darkness robs my joy subtly.

Yet quietly I close my eyes again to sleep.

So You Say (07/22/01)

You say you "love" me
But how could that be?
If this is true, tell me why
All I ever do is cry?
Tell me how love means pain
Where all my energy is drained
I once believed you loved me
How could I be so blind to see?
Life became a constant strain
With few pleasures or gain
You say you "love" me
So why am I so lonely?

Smile and Walk for Me! (11/17/98)

Smile for me and help me smile;
I watch your eyes in subtle view
Expand upon my face.
A gestured smile twinkles thereupon.
Expression holds deep inside my thoughts,
But a smile lies upon my heart.

Walk for me and help me walk;
I watch you move with quick precision.
I chase the shadows in their flight
Until, one day, the shadows...
Are my own.

Sonnet 1 (04/24/01)

You're someone special in my life
You mean so much more than you know
My heart may stop and skip a beat
But dreams of you revive its flow
Mellow, warm, soft, and tenderly sweet
This makes my life feel quite complete.

I feel a strength and realize love
A deep intense conditioning
My breath gasps air within the heart
Lends itself to my positioning
Faith and hope give life a new start
This is the lesson you have taught.

Each day new hope of living life
Gives me strength to love without strife.

Starting Over (05/24/05)

Six months it took to feel some positive change of starting over
The trials and tribulations of everyday uncertainties
Self-pity and determination paired with simple joy and minor depression
It seemed as though each motion of advance slid me further back
Time wore through the shield of patience and filled the hole with absolute desperation
Tear-soaked pillows became my best friend all through the lonely nights
Throughout, I prayed consistently for The Lord's Divine Intervention in my life
You'd think it would be so easy starting over from scratch
New place clear across the country away from the spoils of war
But somehow, no matter how hard I try, the past continues to haunt me
Starting over wasn't as easy or as automatic as I had hoped
But still, I engage my every strength to empower me to be strong
Until one day, I have arrived at the true door to starting over
Six months gone past, I know not where, as I smile looking back from the other side of the door.

Stuck in a Rut (11/17/98)

I'm not into the nineties,
I'm stuck in the seventies.
I'm not into the freedom,
I'm stuck in a rut.

I'm not into floating romances,
I'm not stuck in singular.
I'm not into the freedom,
I'm stuck in a rut.

I'm not into bittersweet goodbyes,
I'm stuck on long hellos.
I'm not into the freedom,
I'm stuck in a rut.

The Aftermath (09/30/04)

Three years have passed since Emancipation Day
Lonely days and nights too many to keep track
Still on a vicious cycle, trying to find my way
Endless moments of sadness that fill my heart
Tears that stain my pillow night after night
When will this feeling pass?
When will I have my new start?
The hope of a new beginning was declared
Strongly and passionately, I reached my goal
So why if I have reached my goal do I feel so weird?
My eyes opened to a new reality
Reflections of past sins unearth themselves for view
Giving way to the path of pure simplicity.

The Haunting (05/17/15)

Lost in the recesses of your mind
Are all the memories of past you'll find
Buried so deeply to not be known
Painful thoughts that you refuse to own
Unearthed memories constantly taunting
With nowhere to escape all the haunting.

The Shadows (07/19/01)

For some unknown reason, I find myself
  in a dark, forsaken place.
A voice calls out to me, "It's your fault,"
  as I try to answer back.
This place I am, I've been before,
  quite often I'm afraid
A dark, cold, and angry place
  where shadows are its walls.
The shadows move in quiet pace
  engulfing all of me.
Then suddenly my breath is gone, I struggle
  just to breathe.
Consumed with anger and then with rage,
  my heart starts to race
I cry out loud, "You did this to me," and
  weep incessantly.
Then in a moment my soul cries out,
  "Lord, help me, please!"
My eyes look beyond the walls, and my soul
  takes me there.
Beyond the walls of shadows is a light
  of peace and hope.
I pray to heaven never to visit
  the dark, forsaken place
And that all the walls within me
  cease to exist
So only light will shine deep within my soul.

Time Has Come (12/17/12)

The time has come
My day's begun
The tasks are new
To do a few
Loans approved or loans denied
Mind open wide
To catch my ride
It's time to work
So don't be a jerk
Get up and take your ass to work!

Trust (02/07/07)

Trust—what is it? Where does it come from?
All our lives, we expect it
When we don't have it, we're always looking for it
Then when it's present, it's taken for granted and questioned
Trust is not inherited, nor is it promised

Where does it go when it no longer exists?
Does it hide behind a corner or hide among our fears?
Does it lurk behind excitement or laugh at every tear?
Trust is simple but absolute.
Trust is peace to relax and just enjoy.

Valiant Victim (07/04/06)

Vaulted visions are the vantage of our valedictions.
Each vision visits a vast vacuum in our hearts.
Veil vague vision to vegetative state
Vacant valleys swell with vandalism validating greed.
Volumes of valuables vanish,
Vanity is vaporized.
Valleys of victims vacate.
Victims, now survivors, view visions of victory
Voice vigorously a valid venture...
Value LIFE deVine!

When They're Gone! (12/24/13)

We think we have it all together; we are strong enough to go about our day without a care or worry. Then suddenly, we feel as though the rug has been pulled out from under our feet. Humbled by default to acknowledge we feel lost, empty, something missing with no resolution. Thumbing through our thoughts to find something we can grasp on to other than ourselves. It does not work to fill the hole that is deep within. We find ourselves running from the thoughts that seem to haunt us, except it's like being chased in your dreams, and your mind is telling you that you're running, but you actually are stuck in one place.

Yes, you finally admit that the reason you are totally feeling unbalanced is because someone you love is no longer there. You cannot get a reassuring hug, rest your head on their shoulder, or tell them your tale for the day. They are NOT there! You actually miss them like you never thought you would. It hurts to just give thought to their absence though you pause to give way to a smile in remembrance of one of the tales they shared.

Within the smile is a yearning to be in their presence. Your heart aches with desire to just be held again, to see their smile, to hear their laughter, and to know they are there. Unfortunately, they are gone! Now you truly know how much love you have for them. It's not that you didn't know before that you loved them, but somehow, that love intensified in their absence.

Just remember to never waste a moment in time to acknowledge in the here and now how much you love them before "they're gone."

Where Are You? (04/26/89)

The dark is all around me
The night has fallen hard
My eyes are playing tricks on me
I think I see the sun.
The shadows that are cast
Never seem to move away
The light is getting brighter
But it's only just a dream.
The dream moves on and on
Then without a warning
I'm in a strange, familiar place
My skin grows cold, my heart pounds fast
I know not why, but this cannot last
A figure appears that comes toward me
And then abruptly stops
Unknown to me, its presence draws me closer
I reach arm's length to see its face
It's you! And then you disappear
I turned in anxiousness to seek you out
But only awoke to an alarm clock.
Where Are You?

Why? (02/28/05)

Days have come and gone, holiday to holiday
Never once stopping to say hello.
Piercing rays of light enter, flirt with each waking day
With little to no chance to grow.

Nights go on in sleeplessness forever
Leaving one in constant limbo.
Dotted skies of twinkling light, dance in whisper
With little to no chance to sow.

Why can't I seem to catch sleep and run in the sun?

Your Loving Child (11/03/06)

Don't cry, Mommy, Daddy
You did real good.
You fed me, clothed me, and kept me warm.

Don't cry, Mommy, Daddy
You can see me in your dreams
You can feel me in your heart.

Don't cry, Mommy, Daddy
You gave me life so grand
You gave me love so much.

Don't cry, Mommy, Daddy
I had all I ever needed
I had YOU!

Words

Some words make you smile
Some words lift your spirit
Some words have you stuck awhile
You feel like you've been bit
Some words make you laugh
Some words expand your mind
Some words make a photograph
Seldom stay behind
Some words stay forever
Influencing us whenever
Words can be good or bad
Can be an enemy or comrade
Don't let words control you
You control the words

How Old Is Too Old? (07/06/20)

To do what you want to do
To learn what you want to learn
To go where you want to go
To love who you want to love
How old is too old?
To find a new love
To change your outlook on life
To be all that you can be
To teach others what you've come to know
How old is too old?
To play in the playground
To swing high on a swing
To glide across the ice on skates
To dance to your heart's content
How old is too old?
Who dictates the age
Requirements?
Who decides laughing out loud
is improper at your age?
What determines whether sexual feelings cannot exist?
Who decides if you can experience deep passions of love?
How old is too old?
How dare anyone decide for you what makes you feel the
way you do
If love and passion excite your soul
Who are they to tell you that you're too old?
The two of us are sublime

A New Day (06/25/20)

Every day is even more amazing than the day before
Why, because we opened our eyes for a new day
Amid all the uncertainties and challenges we're faced with each new day,
The one thing we have is hope.
Hope to breathe,
Hope to smile,
Hope to laugh,
Hope to live another day.
These times are difficult to swallow the reality of so many dying from hatred and illness of
disease of heart, spirit, and body.
We cry out in pain to lose yet another.
But we MUST not give way to despair or live in *fear*,
We MUST continue *to look forward to a new day*!

Appreciation (07/31/17)

Why do we acknowledge and show our respect?
The feelings that are born with their effect
We must take the time to give special thanks
It's like making a deposit to our emotional banks
It should be all of our obligation
To understand showing our admiration
For all of us receiving to contribute
And, without a doubt, show true tribute!

Daddy Hits Mommy, I Don't Know Why (11/18/15)

Daddy hits Mommy, I don't know why
All I know is it makes us cry
Daddy hits Mommy, I don't know why
We try very hard to be good
But no matter, it's never as it should
Daddy hits Mommy, I don't know why
We run and hide and shake with fear
Afraid Daddy may be coming near
Daddy hits Mommy, I don't know why
Quiet, we are to not be heard
Screams from Mommy, but not a word
We peek for Mommy to look and see
Why Daddy hits Mommy, what could it be?
Daddy hits Mommy, I don't know why
Frustrated and sad, we begin to sigh
Daddy hits Mommy, I don't know why
Sometimes he's yelling words I don't know
Other times, it's his fist he will show
Holes in walls, doors all locked, bruises all over
Mommy would use makeup to try to cover
Daddy hits Mommy, I don't know why
Maybe he's mixed up, or maybe he's mad
All I know is that we're all very sad.

PTSD (11/20/15)

I smile, I laugh, all is good
Birds do fly, birds do sing
Everything is as it should
I'm fine, doing my thing
Triggers pressed, emotions change
Smile is gone, hard to breathe
No longer happy, feel strange
Feeling ashamed, time to grieve
No one understands the pain
No one understands me
Questioning if I am sane
Why won't they let me be?
Don't they know I need a hug?
Don't they know I need love?
Bring me out from the hole I've dug
Please embrace this wounded dove!

Destined to Be (08/01/21)

Years ago, a child was born to me
Twins it was and a son to be
This son was all I prayed him to become
A man of grace, patience, and love
Truly a gift from heaven above
She won his love, but from the first he knew
So happy am I for the love they found
The two together they were crowned
He made her his Queen, and she made him her King
Both are quite keen on what each would bring
With marriage they join in trust, faith
They will hold as a must
Love will endure as I foresee
This union was destined to be

About the Author

Shereema often sat on the windowsill of her room, looking out at all the people coming and going, at the city buses that went by on the street where she grew up, as she listened to the sounds of the children playing below her window. At night, she would gaze at the stars from the view of her window. She would imagine herself in the perfect setting of Bedford-Stuyvesant, where she grew up roller-skating around the circle of the projects, then relaxing in the circle on the benches, listening to smooth jazz on her favorite radio station. Music, jazz, and calypso were deep within her spirit.

Shereema was not like the other neighborhood children; she loved music and writing. Shereema loved listening to her great-grandmother tell stories of growing up in Barbados. Shereema's grandmother was born in Barbados but grew up in New York City. At sixteen, she won a scholarship to the Juilliard School.

Shereema would write stories of peace and harmony as a child, imagining the world to be a better place.

CPSIA information can be obtained
at www.ICGtesting.com
Printed in the USA
BVHW041414050423
661805BV00003B/375